The Good, The Bad, and The Wise

Haley Smith

BookLeaf Publishing

Presentation by *BookLeaf Publishing*

Web: www.bookleafpub.com

E-mail: info@bookleafpub.com

ISBN: 9789357213486

First edition 2023

This book is dedicated to the younger me who bottled everything in and never thought her words meant anything. Cheers to letting it all out!

ACKNOWLEDGEMENT

I would not be able to get my work done without the continual support, encouragement, and unconditional love from my husband, Alex Smith. A huge thank you goes out to him for keeping me in check, listening to my rants, and always knowing how to shed light and love on a situation with his goofiness and big heart.

I know I wouldn't be here today without my loving parents, Gary and Laura Thompson, and their support and push to follow my dreams with school and softball by putting in the work to make things happen. They instilled the values and ethics within me that have gotten me this far and I cannot express how grateful I am for them all they have done for me.

My brother, Vincent Thompson, aka: Bubby, helped the younger me get through some emotionally challenging times. A huge thank you to him for being my best friend growing up and for being one of the most humble people I know. He also attended many of my "make-believe school" sessions growing up, which led me to my passion and career today—He should practically have his PhD now!

My grandparents, Don and Mary Bitzel, have always encouraged and cheered me on from school, to softball, to teaching. Countless thank yous go to them for the grit, perseverance, and faith they've instilled in me along the way.

My grandmother, Elaine Thompson, has supported me in all that I have done and I cannot thank her enough for the faith and calming presence that she has spread to me, helping me get this far.

My parents-in-law, Tim and Paula Smith, have truly been like a second set of parents to me, and not many can say that. They have encouraged and guided me through their advice and love that helped me through some tough times. Much gratitude goes to them!

PREFACE

Poems are our deepest thoughts and feelings conducted into rhythmic symphonies that sometimes make all the sense and others none at all. I believe that if a poem is meant to speak to you in that very moment, then it'll be clear as day.

I hope that the love, growth, self-doubt, and struggles within me resonate with you after reading my own rhythmic symphonies.

Unknown

What happens to unsaid words, kept in?
Do they stay bottled within?
Or do they unravel like frayed ribbon into the
wind?

What about broken dreams?
Do they eventually reconvene?
Or do they shatter like a mirror into a reflective
defeat?

And how about a lost soul?
Does it ever regain control?
Or does it wonder like a rabbit into a spiraling,
black hole?

And what happens to the memories?
Are they remembered for centuries?
Or do they get tossed on a mantel as a
meaningless accessory?

What happens to a decaying carcass?
Does it disintegrate into dust?
Or does it come back with vengeance to haunt
us?

Maybe we just aren't meant to know?
Whatever happens to the mysterious unknown,
I can only hope they aren't alone.

Everything Happens for a Reason

The darkness steals the daylight earlier each day,
leaving only slivers of golden rays that peak
through shadowed trees.
Warm hues of crimson, gold, and amber
suffocate the olive tones.
Chilled nights and blistering winds kidnap the
withering, changing leaves with just a breeze.

"Follow me," they said, as they whirled, twirled,
and whooshed into the sky.
More and more leaves began to follow the same
whirling, twirling, and whooshing pattern as the
days grew shorter and the nights grew colder.

The last leaf lulled into the wind and landed
upon the brown bed of decay.
The warm hues had faded as summer's harvest
had dissipated.

It felt as if last winter's colorless
emptiness was meaningless;
As if spring's flower buds had never bloomed;
As if summer's sun hadn't grown a thing;
It felt as if the Earth had seemingly been

interrupted…

…paused...

The barren trees contemplate their purpose;
for what good comes of vulnerability?
What good comes of being exposed and unsure
of what the future holds?
The trees mumbled amongst each other,
unwittingly, of what would soon unfold.

Little did the trees know, they'd soon be
stronger, fuller and more beautiful than before;
Their branches would no longer be iced over and
numb if they'd just wait for the months to come.
Everything happens for a reason-
even the changing of the seasons.
When the leaves say, "follow me!"
It's truly meant to be.

Carousel of Life

Lost in the roundabout
Day in and day out
Sun up and sun down
Around and around
The carousel of life we go-

The hustle and bustle
A piece of the puzzle
Plant and grow
Go with the flow
On the carousel of life we go-

Flashing lights- a blur-
The music connoisseur
Moving perpetually
A stop, eventually,
Waiting to slow
On the carousel of life we go-

Spinning and jumping has stopped-
Stealing time right off the clock
Forgetting to enjoy the little things
The carousel of life had to bring
Troubles came and passed
Changing the scenery, at last

Where we will go, nobody knows-
Off the carousel of life we go-

A Bad Day

I know you're having a bad day,
and that's totally okay.
Everybody has them-
It's going to happen.
Don't worry about this one crappy moment.
How is this one any different?
You've made it through all the others,
and you'll certainly have another.
But look at all you've come back from!
Your rear-view mirror sees how far you've
come.
The past seems closer than it appears,
but the present is much more clear.
Take a deep breath, count to ten,
and come back to a good day once again!

Full

Does stress ever soak into your insides like
you're a sudsy sponge;
All at once and into a plunge?
Do they fill your pores and weigh you down,
waiting for your thoughts and emotions to
drown?

A soaked and sudsy sponge can't execute the
chore.
It is simply too full, full to its core.
It must be drained when there's no room for
more.
It's definitely not something to ignore.

You've bitten off more than you can chew,
so here's what you should do…
Free yourself from the weight of the world
and force that sudsy sponge to hurl.
Sometimes life is more clear in a drought,
so be sure to wring yourself out.

It's okay to take a step back
when you feel like you're about to crack.
Walk away and say, "No thanks, I'm full…
…I'm bursting at the seams and out of my
skull!"

Focus

I’m not only a message in a bottle-
I am one million messages, full to the throttle.
Simple thoughts or taxing tasks,
it gets hard to stay on track!
Trying to focus on one thing right
is like a cat playing with two strings.

Growing Pains

Stop allowing negativity to fill your time-
Only positive things will make you shine.
Don't let the pessimist cloud your mind-
A hope for sunnier days is better, you'll find.
Refrain from those who always complain
and who use the Lord's name in vein.
Don't let them take advantage of your kindness,
for the fear of disappointment can blinds us.
Avoid those who fail to fill you up
and search for those who will fill your cup.
And, darling, if you want to go grow,
you've got to learn to let it go.

A Vacation

A ticket
A ride
A trip

A picture
A memory
A blip

A family
A laugh
A skip

A moment
A pause
A memory

His Backpack

His backpack was a reflection of his own-
A deep, daring ocean waiting for him to drown.
And the more he carried it on his back,
the more it weighed him down.

The torn papers of abandonment holding onto
the hope of being together again;
The mismatched gloves of divorce replacing a
married match of a mother and a father;
The scattered wrappers of emotion breaking free
like an opened cage of commotion;
The broken pencils of rage waiting to be used
for revenge…

His backpack was a reflection of his own-
Busting at the seams and barely keeping him
afloat.

TheatEarth

Have you ever looked into a midday sky?
And I mean, really look up high…
Narrow in, focus hard, and watch the clouds go
by.
Isn't it weird that you never see the stars beyond
that bright blue barrier?
Like a message sent and delivered by the mail
carrier,
the entire Earth changes scenes from its exterior!
From dusk to dawn
the curtain is drawn
and the next act is up.

The Seasons of Life

At first it's cold and harsh like the winter blues
Then Summer's harvest announces that change is due
Finally, fall's foliage proclaims that change is beautiful in the end
Seasons change in phases, just like people do

How Dare You?

How dare you blare your wretched sounds at
me!
How dare you sink my heart in slumber; a ship
at sea!
How dare you demand me of my immediate
removal!
How dare you torture me with a seal of
disapproval!
How dare you hold me prisoner to your whole
numbers!
How dare you flash like falling, red embers!

All you do is sit there and mock!
How dare you, alarm clock!

Therapy Beach

Careless and worry-free on the beach-
I lie underneath a feathered palm tree.
Scents of sea salt in the ocean breeze-
I don't know when I'd ever felt so at ease.

The highs and lows of the ocean waves
resemble the good and bad of our days.
Troubles and triumphs will come and go,
like seasons passing from sun to snow.

The warmth from the sun gives me chills-
My reddened skin turns fried and grilled.
The melatonin is released and instilled-
I am officially addicted to being refilled.

The sand exfoliates my feet and toes-
A silky, smoothen layer now exposed.
The steps I walked have decomposed-
Onto the next adventure, I go!

I Have and Haven't

I have both run out of time
and had none left to spare.
I have done everything I could
and done nothing to prepare.
I have spoken what's on my mind
and felt completely impaired.
I have both checked everything off my list
and sat there and stared.
I wonder the answer to this issue
and sometimes I really don't wish to.

I Became the Song

My thoughts drowned into the rhythm that the
song left behind in my patterned tracks.
I became numb to my surroundings.
I became blind to the scenery.
I became the song.
Note by note,
beat by beat,
I was the song.
Each footstep generated another beat of the song
swirling into an endless delirium.
Walking into the next song,
as if time had warped,
the clock struck the next hour.
The words filled my soul deep from within
and from my toes to my chin,
I became the song.

I Will Not

I will not let you spit those twisted words into
my face
I will not let your knife slice into my back in
disgrace
I will not let your comments contaminate inside
of me
I will not let your shoe imprint on the front of
me
I will not let your daggering eyes pierce into
mine
I will not let you have control over my mind

Suitcase

We all have a suitcase.
Some are are hard-shelled
and can withstand a drop.
Others cave in from just a yell.
And have a rough story to tell.
Some don't know where to begin
or even know where all they've been.
I think a big part of this life
is knowing that we all have a suitcase
different than the one we have to face.

Good Ol' Days

Isn't it ironic how we don't know we're in the
good ol' days until they're gone?
It's like eating cake with a blindfold on.
One minute, life is sugary and sweet,
and the next we're dropping to our knees-
We pray for the days that once were,
and ignore the fact that "the end" would soon
occur.

I just wish I had a remote—
One that could replay the memories
that meant the most…

Like getting groceries and giggling with mom
as she'd cheered me up when I was sad,
and throwing ball in the backward with dad.
Playing pretend school with my brother and
cousin,
even though they felt like it was just a prison.

I just wish I had a remote—
One that could rid the resentful times: revoked.
One that could pause a moment in time
like when we were kids in the summertime.

One that can show us the things we took for
granted and missed;
I'm sure I'd have a whole list.

Grace

When you're stuck between a rock and a hard
place,
barely breathing and blue in the face,
just remember to give yourself some grace
no matter what decision you make.
No matter what you do,
It'll probably upset a person or two.
The one you need to worry about is you.

The Little Things

The end of dinner is just the beginning.
We save our forks and wait while grinning.
Grandma brings out her pound cake
that took her hours to bake!

Shaking Grandpa's hand is always rewarding!
He empties his pockets of change he'd been
hoarding.
He'll pass it to us in a handshake
For getting good grades.

Hugging my husband right after work is so
comforting,
even though his face looks like he's losing air
and suffering.
Although he would probably never say,
that's also his favorite part of the day!

When the summer sun beats on my skin and
makes me tingle,
that means it's entered my heart and will soon
rekindle.
The flame of happiness within will be ablaze,
all thanks to those golden rays.

Life really is about the little things
and looking forward to what each day will bring.

Alive

Hopeless from defeat and longing for revival,
I set sail for the one mom told me to find.
Carrying every heartache and heartbreak,
a doubt of redemption danced into my mind.

You swam right to my line,
knocked me off my feet,
and noticed my tethered heart—
Shattered, torn, battered and beat.

You mended my heart with yours
with such understanding and grace.
That's when two became one,
consuming the same space.

Like a breath of fresh, summer air
You made me feel alive.
After fighting that battle alone,
I'm the one who's been revived.

www.ingramcontent.com/pod-product-compliance
Lightning Source LLC
Chambersburg PA
CBHW051752130826
49812CB00033B/1122
9789357213486